INUYASHA

VOL. 13

Story and Art by
RUMIKO TAKAHASHI

Translation/Mari Morimoto
Touch-Up Art & Lettering/Wayne Truman & Bill Schuch
Cover Design/Hidemi Sahara
Graphics & Design/Sean Lee
Editor/Julie Davis

Production Manager/Nobi Watanabe
Managing Editor/Annette Roman
Editor-in-Chief/William Flanagan
VP of Marketing/Liza Coppola
Sr. VP of Editorial/Hyoe Narita
Publisher/Seiji Horibuchi

Printed in Canada.

Published by VIZ, LLC
P.O. Box 77010
San Francisco, CA 94107

10 9 8 7 6 5 4
First printing, March 2003
Second printing, April 2003
Third printing, July 2003
Fourth printing, January 2004

store.viz.com

www.viz.com

INUYASHA

VOL. 13

STORY AND ART BY

RUMIKO TAKAHASHI

CONTENTS

SCROLL ONE
KIKYO'S ARROW
7

SCROLL TWO
WHERE IS THE IMP?
25

SCROLL THREE
KIKYO CAPTURED
43

SCROLL FOUR
DEATH BY ILLUSION
61

SCROLL FIVE
DEATH WISH
79

SCROLL SIX
NARAKU'S TRUE FORM
97

SCROLL SEVEN
TOTO-SAI, THE SWORDSMITH
117

SCROLL EIGHT
TENSEIGA
135

SCROLL NINE
SCAR OF THE WIND
153

SCROLL TEN
THE INVISIBLE PATH
171

Long ago, in the "Warring States" era of Japan's Muromachi period (*Sengoku-jidai*, approximately 1467-1568 CE), a legendary doglike half-demon called "Inu-Yasha" attempted to steal the Shikon Jewel, or "Jewel of Four Souls," from a village, but was stopped by the enchanted arrow of the village priestess, Kikyo. Inu-Yasha fell into a deep sleep, pinned to a tree by Kikyo's arrow, while the mortally wounded Kikyo took the Shikon Jewel with her into the fires of her funeral pyre. Years passed.

Fast forward to the present day. Kagome, a Japanese high school girl, is pulled into a well one day by a mysterious centipede monster, and finds herself transported into the past, only to come face to face with the trapped Inu-Yasha. She frees him, and Inu-Yasha easily defeats the centipede monster.

The residents of the village, now fifty years older, readily accept Kagome as the reincarnation of their deceased priestess Kikyo, a claim supported by the fact that the Shikon Jewel emerges from a cut on Kagome's body. Unfortunately, the jewel's rediscovery means that the village is soon under attack by a variety of demons in search of this treasure. Then, the jewel is accidentally shattered into many shards, each of which may have the fearsome power of the entire jewel.

Although Inu-Yasha says he hates Kagome because of her resemblance to Kikyo, the woman who "killed" him, he is forced to team up with her when Kaede, the village leader, binds him to Kagome with a powerful spell. Now the two grudging companions must fight to reclaim and reassemble the shattered shards of the Shikon Jewel before they fall into the wrong hands.

THIS VOLUME An impossible fight, the demon Naraku revived, and the secrets of Inu-Yasha's sword

CHARACTERS

INU-YASHA
A half-human, half-demon hybrid son of a human mother and a demon father, Inu-Yasha has the claws of a demon, a thick mane of white hair, and ears rather like a dog's. The necklace he wears carries a powerful spell that allows Kagome to control him with a single word. Thanks to his human half, Inu-Yasha's powers are different from those of full-blooded monsters—a fact that the Shikon Jewel has the power to change.

KIKYO
A powerful priestess, Kikyo was charged with the awesome responsibility of protecting the Shikon Jewel from demons and humans who coveted its power. She died after firing the enchanted arrow that kept Inu-Yasha imprisoned for fifty years.

KAGOME
Working with Inu-Yasha to recover the shattered shards of the Shikon Jewel, Kagome routinely travels into Japan's past through an old, magical well on her family's property. All this time travel means she's stuck with living two separate lives in two centuries. Will she *ever* be able to catch up to her schoolwork?

SESSHO-MARU
Inu-Yasha's half-brother is a full demon who hates his half-breed younger brother and covets his sword, the Tetsusaiga, a legacy from their demon father.

NARAKU
An enigmatic demon, Naraku is the one responsible for both Miroku's curse and for turning Kikyo and Inu-Yasha against one another for reasons that are as yet unknown.

MIROKU
An easygoing Buddhist priest (also somewhat of a ladies' man), Miroku carries a "hellhole" in his hand, a curse that was originally inflicted on his grandfather by the demon Naraku.

SANGO
A "Demon Exterminator" from the village where the Shikon Jewel was first born, Sango lost her father and little brother to a demon attack arranged by the mysterious Naraku.

SCROLL ONE

KIKYO'S ARROW

KIKYO...
WHY IS SHE HERE ?!
AND...
WHAT WILL INU-YASHA DO WHEN HE SEES HER?
OH!
HHOOOOOO
VSSH
LORD MIROKU !
LADY... KAGOME... ?

WHERE'S INU-YASHA?
ARE YOU ALL RIGHT?
HOW IS IT...THAT YOU ARE SO UNAFFECTED BY THIS MIASMA... OF EVIL...?
OH...!
HHOOOOOOO

SSHHH
GGGH...
HEH HEH HEH... THE WOMAN... SHE AIN'T HUMAN, EH?
THEN I'LL MAKE HER PART OF ME...
KIKYO ?!
!
HHOOOOO

DON'T YOU DARE TOUCH KIKYO--!
VSH
JABB

KIKYO
!
FWAAH
RRRR...
BZZZZ
BLIK
BLIK
!
OOM
ZZZZZZ
HWAH
NGH!
DONK
KARARA

YOU-- !
SSHHHH
DON'T LOSE YOUR TEMPER, INU-YASHA !
IF YOU DEFEAT HIM, YOUR BODY WILL BE TAKEN OVER BY THE POISON IMP...!
SHUT UP!
!

...
KAGOME...
WHOA!
KRONG
BLAST IT.
MY ONLY CHOICE IS TO FIGHT!
LORD MIROKU... WHAT IS A "POISON IMP"?
IF HE FIGHTS WITHIN THIS ARENA...
WHETHER HE WINS OR LOSES, HIS BODY WILL FUSE WITH THAT OF THE DEMON'S.

OH... !
LADY KAGOME, WHAT ARE YOU DOING... !
I'VE GOT TO...
...GET KIKYO'S BODY TO A SAFE PLACE !
IF I DON'T, INU-YASHA...

WILL
CONTINUE
FIGHTING THAT
DEMON, IN
ORDER TO
PROTECT
HER...
ZASH

BECAUSE
INU-YASHA
WILL NEVER
ABANDON
KIKYO!

I HATE IT, BUT...
KIKYO!
ZZZZZ
SHHOOO
...
ARE YOU AWAKE?!
CAN YOU STAND?!
DNK
GG...
YOU!

VVVN
!
DOK
WATCH OUT!
KARARARA
FWA
HUH...?
FOOL...
INU-YASHA HAS LOST HIS REASON....
NOW THAT YOU'VE SHOWN UP...

YOU MONSTER !!
OOOOOHH
FSSHH
IF HE KILLS HIM...
NO!

KRAK
KZZZZZZZ
!
WOBBLE...

SSHHHHH
WOBBLE...
OOOOOHH
KIKYO...

KRAK
FSSH
ZZZZ
HWOOO
!
THE EVIL AURA THAT FILLED THE AIR....
IS DISSI-PATING!
THE SPELL... IS BROKEN...!
GGWOOOO

RRRRRMMMMMMM
!
GLUB
GLUB
GLUB
WHAT...
!
HOOOOOOO
HHWOOO
?
ZT
ZT
ZT
ZT

HOOOOO
!
EEEE...!

WE'RE BEING DRAGGED ALONG ?!

SCROLL TWO

WHERE IS THE IMP?

FSSSH
THEY'RE BEING SUCKED OUT!
HOOOOOOO
INU-YASHA!
LADY KAGOME!

SSHH
UGH!
!
SSHH
INU-YASHA!
KAGOME!

GRIP
ARE YOU ALL RIGHT ?!
WHERE'S KIKYO ?!
!
SSHH
KIKYO !
SSHH

WHOOOOOOOOO
!

FFFSSSSS
NARAKU ?!
NARAKU HAS A BODY... ?!
BUT I THOUGHT MY ARROW DISINTEGRATED IT LAST TIME...

SSSHHHHH
HSSS

I'LL TEAR YOU APART!
YOU'RE THE ONE WHO SPELLED US...!
YOU...
BRRROK

FWAP
THAT BODY...
IS A KUGUTSU -- FOR A PUPPET MASTER!
SHRRRRRR R
FWAP
MMGGG
KRAK KRAK KRAK
FFFF

ZP ZP
ZP ZP
ZP
ZP
EH...
?!
BEK BEK BEK

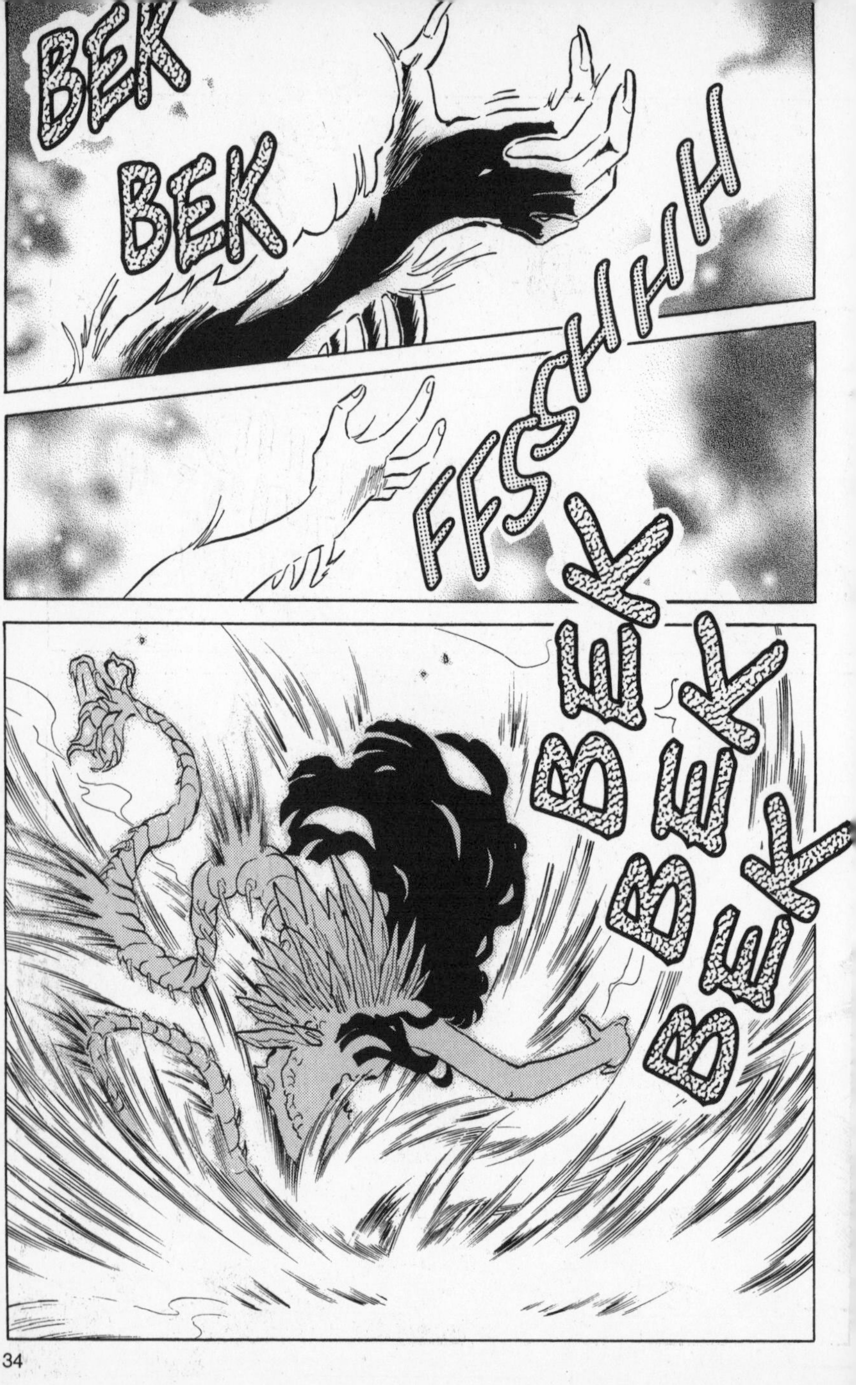
BEK
BEK
FFSSHHH
BEK
BEK
BEK

RRGH...!
SSHHH
THE DEMON... IT'S BEING SUCKED INTO NARAKU'S BODY...?!
NARAKU--!
SHHHHP
A SHIELD!
BEK BEK
SHAH

SSHHOOOOO
SSHHHH
RRRM...
FEH... YOU TWO...
YOU WERE DRAWN TO THE MOUNTAIN'S EVIL AURA AND FOUND YOURSELVES CAUGHT UP IN MY LITTLE CAVE, EH?
SSSZZZZ

THAT DEMON... THE POISON IMP...
WAS CREATED TO BECOME NARAKU'S NEW BODY ?!
!
SSHHH
KIKYO !!

...THIS WOMAN SUNDERED THE SPELL FROM WITHIN, HM?
THANKS TO HER I HAVE THIS BODY.
SHE WAS A LOYAL SERVANT INDEED.
WHAT... !
THAT'S A LIE!
IF KIKYO ***HADN'T*** SHOT HER ARROW THEN...
INU-YASHA WOULD HAVE KILLED THE DEMON...
...AND ***HIS*** BODY WOULD HAVE BECOME FUSED WITH THE DEMON'S!

SO KIKYO...
WAS PROTECTING INU-YASHA!
THE KIKYO WHO 50 YEARS AGO FOLLOWED YOU TO HER DEATH, EH...?
THEN IT WOULD SEEM THAT THIS WOMAN TRULY IS...
SHH
NKH!

KEEP YOUR FILTHY HANDS OFF HER!
VSSH
YOU--
BOOF
!
IS THAT... POISON ?!

KIKYO...!
HEH HEH HEH... KIKYO'S MYSTIC POWERS...
ARE TOO PRECIOUS TO HAND OVER TO YOU...
HHOOOOOO
VSSH
UGH!
INU-YASHA...

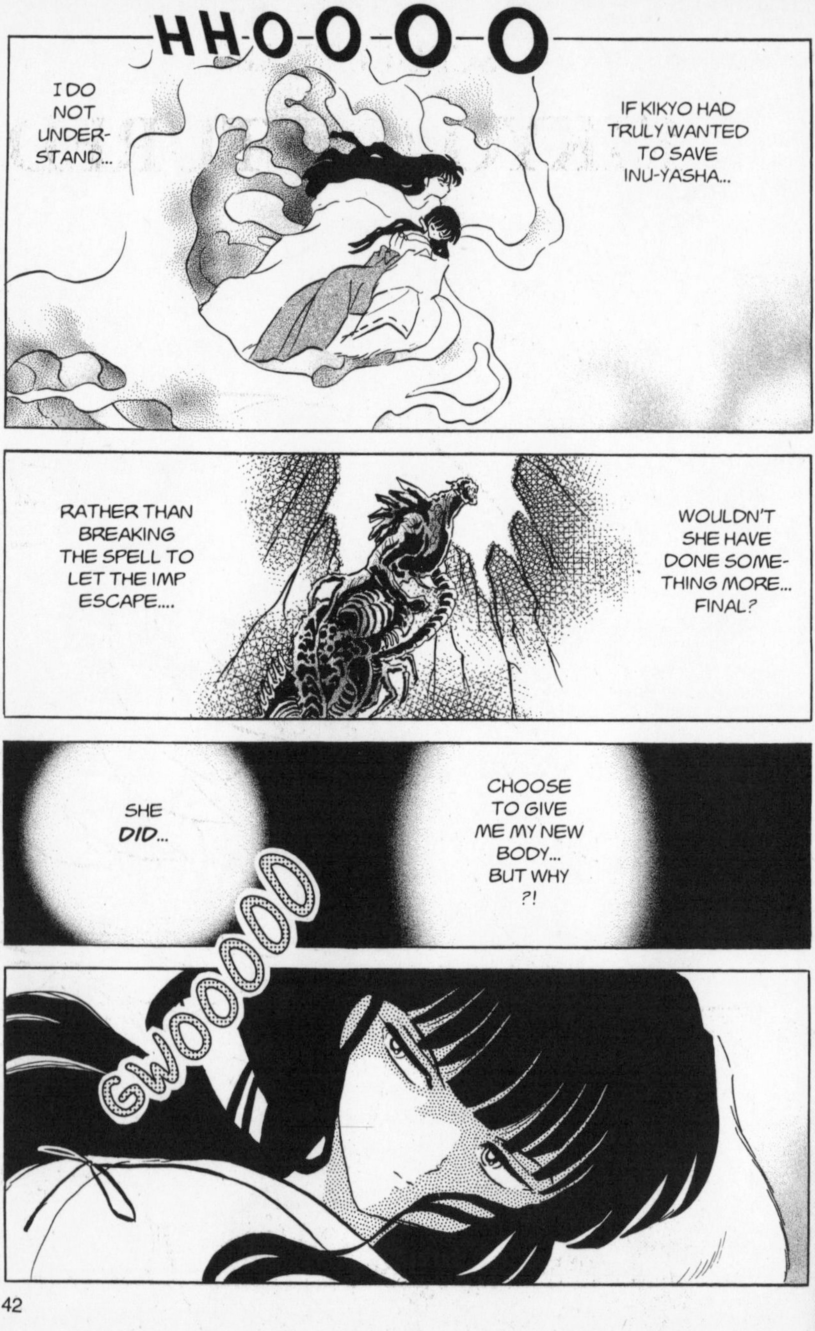
HH-O-O-O-O
I DO NOT UNDER-STAND...
IF KIKYO HAD TRULY WANTED TO SAVE INU-YASHA...
RATHER THAN BREAKING THE SPELL TO LET THE IMP ESCAPE....
WOULDN'T SHE HAVE DONE SOME-THING MORE... FINAL?
SHE *DID*...
CHOOSE TO GIVE ME MY NEW BODY... BUT WHY ?!
GWOOOOOO

SCROLL THREE

KIKYO CAPTURED

HHOOOO
SSHHHH
BXXX
ZZZT
ZXXX
BXXT

ZXXX
BXXX
THOSE VERMIN WON'T BE ABLE TO ENTER.
I'VE RAISED A SHIELD.
IT SEEMS THAT YOU ARE PARALYZED WITHOUT YOUR DEAD SOULS.
SHK

...
WHAT ARE YOU PLOTTING?
WHAT IS IT?
KIKYO...
THIS TIME, YOU WON'T BE ABLE TO ESCAPE.
IF YOU HAD TRULY WANTED TO SAVE INU-YASHA FROM FUSING WITH THAT DEMON'S BODY...
YOUR ARROW PIERCED AND SHATTERED MY SPELL EASILY.

...YOU WOULD HAVE SHOT AT THE DEMON.
HAD YOU DONE SO, IT WOULD HAVE BEEN DISPELLED WITHOUT A TRACE.
I HAD TO KNOW...
WHAT WOULD BE WAITING...
AT THE DEMON'S DESTINATION...
AND THERE... WAS YOU...
YOU'VE BECOME QUITE A MONSTER, EH...
...ONI-GUMO ?

ONI-GUMO... HEH.
WHAT MEMORIES THAT BRINGS.
50 YEARS AGO... HIS LIFE SAVED BY YOU, KIKYO...
...A WOUNDED BANDIT HIDING IN A CAVE...
...WHO OFFERED HIS DAMAGED BODY WILLINGLY TO THE DEMONS...
...TO BE DEVOURED.
USING ONI GUMO'S TAINTED SOUL AS THEIR CRUCIBLE, THE GATHERED DEMONS BECAME ONE....
...AND A NEW DEMON WAS BORN.
HSSH

AND IT WAS HE... WHO LED ME TO MY DEATH 50 YEARS AGO...
"NARAKU"... FEH.
HEH HEH HEH...
INDEED... A SATISFYING REVENGE.
WHAP
WHAP
WHAP
YOU MAY COME IN HANDY AGAIN, KIKYO.
FOR SURELY...

...THE SENTIMENTAL INU-YASHA...
...WOULD NEVER ALLOW HIMSELF TO ABANDON YOU.
HHOOOO
IS IT ME... OR ARE THOSE TWO ACTING STRANGELY...?
THEY ARE.
INU-YASHA...
HEY.
...

LET'S GO.
WE'VE GOT TO RESCUE KIKYO.
YOU GUYS STAY BEHIND.
I'LL GO ALONE...
WHA...
DON'T BE A FOOL, YOU...YOU FOOL!
BOOT
KIKYO WAS KIDNAPPED BY NARAKU!!
INDEED.
THIS IS NOT YOUR PROBLEM ALONE, INU-YASHA.
INU-YASHA,
IF YOU'RE TRYING TO SPARE MY FEELINGS OR SOMETHING, DON'T.
EH...?

KIKYO SAVED YOU...
AND THEN, HER STRENGTH DRAINED, SHE WAS KIDNAPPED BY NARAKU, RIGHT?
WE'RE A TEAM! WE HAVE TO SAVE HER NOW--
WITH NO SNEAKING AROUND!
WHO DO YOU THINK IS "SNEAKING AROUND"...?!
STOP IT-- BOTH OF YOU!
WE HAVE COMPANY....
BZZZZ
THE VENOM WASPS!
SHK

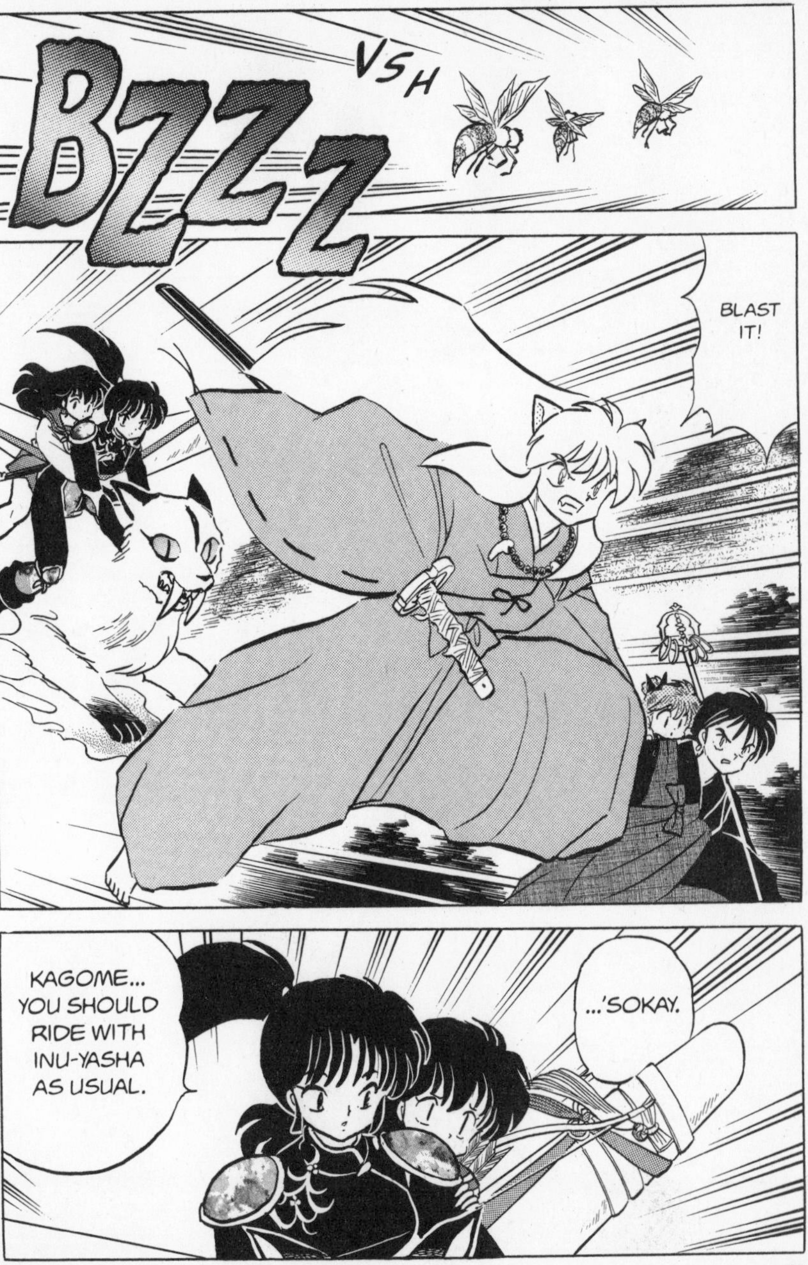
BZZZ
VSH
BLAST IT!
KAGOME... YOU SHOULD RIDE WITH INU-YASHA AS USUAL.
...'SOKAY.

BECAUSE... RIGHT NOW...
...HIS THOUGHTS ARE ALL ON KIKYO.
I SAID SOME PRETTY NOBLE THINGS JUST NOW...
BUT THE TRUTH IS... I AM JEALOUS...
SIGH
...
KIKYO... DIED BECAUSE OF NARAKU!
HWOOO
I CAN'T LET HIM...
TAKE HER AGAIN!

SSHHHHH
!
THESE ARE...
KIKYO'S SOUL SKIMMERS!
SHE MUST NEARBY!
HOOSH
MIST ?!
PFF
NARAKU MAY HAVE A TRAP AHEAD! DON'T LET YOUR GUARD DOWN, INU-YASHA!
I KNOW!

KIKYO
!
HOOOO
HOOOO
?!
KRAKLE KRAKLE
THAT'S...

BE CAREFUL, ALL OF YOU...
!
THEY'RE GONE ?!
SHK
?!
KRAK
KRAKKLE
KRAK
RRROOOR

RRRROO-O-O
KRAKKLE
KRAKKLE
A VILLAGE... ?!
IT'S BEING ATTACKED BY SOMETHING...?!
THERE HE IS! IT'S INU-YASHA!
HE'S AFTER THE SHIKON JEWEL!
HE ATTACKED US!
WHAT... ?!
!
KLATTER

INU-YASHA!
THE SHIKON JEWEL?!
HHOOOOO
KIKYO?!

THIS IS THAT DAY...
50 YEARS AGO...WHEN I WAS KILLED BY KIKYO!!

SCROLL FOUR

DEATH BY ILLUSION

THAT TERRIBLE DAY...
HAVE I GONE BACK TO THAT DAY?!
...WHEN MY KIKYO SHOT ME DEAD...?
THOK

OH...
SHK
INU-YASHA...
KIKYO...
THE SHIKON JEWEL...
FOR SUCH A THING...

...YOU BETRAYED ME...
NO! YOU'RE WRONG, KIKYO!
WE WERE BOTH CAUGHT IN NARAKU'S TRAP!
I **DIDN'T** BETRAY YOU !!
I WAS NAÏVE.
FOR A MOMENT, I IMAGINED I COULD LIVE MY LIFE WITH YOU...
KIKYO...

INU-YASHA...
I WON'T...
LET YOU DIE ALONE...
YES...
SHE FOLLOWED ME...
...FOLLOWED ME IN DEATH.

I UNDERSTAND, KIKYO...
...WE MUST GO TOGETHER...

HHOOOO
WHERE ARE INU-YASHA AND THE OTHERS...?
WHERE AM I...?
!
HHOOOO
THE SOUND OF WIND... FROM THE WIND TUNNEL...?
HHHH
?!
HYOOOOO

HHHHHHH
KRAKKLE
KRAKKLE
KRAKKLE
OH... !
HHOOOOO
I'M GOING TO BE SWALLOWED UP!

HHHHOOOOO
WHERE IS...
EVERY-ONE?
KNCH
!
WHAT... ?!
THEY'RE ALL...
HYUNN

HYUNN
PWAK
THUK
KOHAKU... !
SHK
THANKS, BIG SISTER...
YOU KILLED EVERY-ONE... ?!

HURRY, SISTER...
...COME JOIN ME IN THE NEXT WORLD...
I CAN CONTINUE... AS MY LORD NARAKU COMMANDS.
YOU'VE ALWAYS PROTECTED ME...HAVEN'T YOU?
AND THANKS TO YOU...
THUK
SPURRT
KOHAKU... (!)

SHHHH
BXXT
BZZT
HEH HEH HEH...
ALL EASY MARKS FOR MY "DEATH BY ILLUSION"...

MY, MY...
HOW FRAIL HUMAN HEARTS ARE, INDEED.
SADNESS...
FEAR... CONFUSION...
IF EVEN ONE OF THESE DARK ROOTS REACHES DOWN TO THE RESERVOIRS OF HORROR I'VE SUNK IN THIS LAND, THEN IT'S OVER....
HHHHHH
THE DARK ILLUSION WILL RISE IN THEM...
AND CONSUME THEIR SOULS.
YES, KIKYO...
EVEN YOUR BELOVED INU-YASHA IS QUICKLY ENSNARED BY MY ILLUSIONS.
ONLY--

THAT GIRL KAGOME... AS I SUSPECTED....
...IS IMPERVIOUS TO MY SPELL....
SSSHHHHH
GUYS? WHERE'D YOU GO ...?
HHHOOOO
SHFF
PWAK

JEEZ-- THIS IS SO CREEPY !
I KEEP THINKING THESE VINE-LIKE THINGS ARE MOVING.
SHFF
SHE WALKS THROUGH MY MYSTIC WEB...
...BUT THE STRANDS ARE UNABLE TO SNARE HER AT ALL ...
VPP
PCH
PCH
KIKYO... AND NARAKU!
B-BMP
B-BMP
B-BMP
NARAKU... DOESN'T KNOW I'M HERE?
NOW'S MY CHANCE... !

PLEASE HIT!
SHA
BWANG

THUK
YES ...!
HUH... ?!
I ALREADY KNEW...
THAT YOU WOULD MAKE IT HERE BY YOURSELF...
GOOD WORK.
HEH HEH HEH...

KRIK
KRIK
KRIK
!
RRRMMMM
OH...!
KRAK
KRAK
KRAK
IF I CAN'T DESTROY HER SOUL...
I WILL DESTROY THE FLESH THAT HARBORS IT!

SCROLL FIVE
DEATH WISH

HHHHOOOOO
KRAK KRAK KRAK
UGH...
GLUB GLUB GLUB

WHAP
PWAP
SOME-ONE... PLEASE...!
FWAP FWAP
NO ONE IS GOING TO COME.
HEH HEH HEH...

INU-YASHA AND THE OTHERS' SOULS HAVE BEEN ENSNARED BY MY "DEATH BY ILLUSION" SPELL... AND ARE SOON TO DIE...
SSHFF
I'M GOING TO BE EATEN AWAY... !
BRRR
KLATTER
SIZZLE
THERE IS NO ONE LEFT TO RESCUE YOU!
KLATTER
SHK
HELP...
INU-YASHA-- !

SHK
!
KIKYO ?!

HEH. IF HE'S USING A GOLEM...
SSP...
....NARAKU MUST TRULY FEAR YOU.
SNAP
KRMBL
KRMBL
YOU'RE NOT PARALYZED...?
I COULD HAVE MOVED WHENEVER I WANTED TO.
BUT FIRST...

...I HAD TO KNOW...
...WHAT NARAKU INTENDED.
I SEEMS THAT NARAKU ALSO...
...SEES YOU AS THE GREATEST NUISANCE.
"ALSO"... ?

HSSSH
KIKYO... IF I'D ONLY...
...ONLY TRUSTED YOU...BACK THEN...
INSTEAD, I HATED YOU.
I WAS IMPALED BY YOUR ARROW...
AND I WAS ALONE AGAIN.
ALONE...
I DIDN'T KNOW... THAT YOU FOLLOWED ME INTO DEATH.
INU-YASHA--

INU-YASHA--
YOU'RE NOT ALONE ANY MORE--!
KAGOME--?
WHERE...
WHERE ARE YOU NOW?
GNNG
THAT'S RIGHT--!
I'M INSIDE NARAKU'S TRAP!
KAGOME...
WHERE IS KAGOME?!

WELL, INU-YASHA.
SO YOU'VE COME TO TREASURE YOUR LIFE, EH?
GRRN
KI... KYO!
RRR
I MET KAGOME...
...AND REGAINED THE SOUL THAT I'D LOST.
I...
I CAN'T LET HER DIE HERE...
SOMEDAY, I'LL GO WHERE YOU ARE, KIKYO!
BUT THAT ISN'T **TODAY**!
KRAK

PAK
PAK
PAK
PAK
!
GRRNNN
KRAKLE
KRAKLE
KRAKLE

KRAKLE
KRAKLE
KRAKLE
EVERYTHING THAT JUST HAPPENED... WAS AN ILLUSION?!
RRROOOOR
SNAP
SNAP
DAMN HIM!
HSSSH
!
HHOOOOO

SSSHHH
GNG GNG GNG
FSSH
MIROKU!
THESE VINES...
ZASH
TMP
M--...
MY ARM...!

MIROKU!
SNAP OUT OF IT!
SHGG
!
EH...?
MY WIND TUNNEL...
IT WAS SWALLOWING MY WHOLE BODY...
HE'S...
TERRIFIED?!
THESE ILLUSIONS!
THEY CHOOSE YOUR BIGGEST FEAR.
MIROKU, YOU GO LOOK FOR SANGO.
SHE MUST BE CAUGHT BY THE VINES' ILLUSIONS TOO.
BUT WHERE'S KAGOME?!
SSHHH

VSH
WHERE'S KAGOME ?!
SSHHHLLRR
SSHHH
RROOOOR
...
WHAT- ?!
WHAT- ?!
SSHHHLLRR
S-SHHHH
HUH... ?

!
WAFT
SHE'S... ?
... HELPING ME...?
PNG
OH...
CHNK
THE SHIKON SHARD...

H- HEY... WHAT DO YOU THINK YOU'RE...
NOW... YOU MAY RELEASE HER.
IT IS NOT YOURS TO POSSESS.
THE SHIKON JEWEL WAS ORIGINALLY *MINE* TO PROTECT AND PURIFY.
!
FWAH

SHE'S GOING TO LET ME DIE!
KAGOME!

SCROLL SIX
NARAKU'S TRUE FORM

KIKYO...
...DO YOU WANT ME DEAD?!
BAM

SHK
YOU ARE ME.
BUT THERE NEEDS BE ONLY ONE OF US IN THIS REALITY...
KAGOME!
VSH

SHFF
!
SHK
INU-YASHA!
I-...
KAGOME!
WHSH
...

VMM
GNG
ARE YOU ALL RIGHT?!
WHAT IN ALL THE HELLS IS GOING ON HERE?
K-KIKYO WAS...
TRYING TO...
WHAT...
I TOOK THE SHIKON SHARD FROM HER. THAT'S ALL.

KIKYO, YOU...
IT'S BECAUSE SHE'S CARRYING THIS...
...THAT KAGOME'S LIFE IS IN DANGER.
NARAKU, I SUSPECT, WAS PLANNING TO MELT HER BODY...
!
...AND TAKE THE REMAINING SHARDS OF THE JEWEL.
GLUB
H-HEY, WAIT A MINUTE...
IT'S NOT NARAKU WHO'S STEALING THE SHARDS NOW-- IT'S YOU!
SHFF

SHK
KIKYO!
WHERE ARE YOU GOING?!
WAFFT...
SHK
...
HSSSH

...
KAGOME...
WHAT HAPPENED BETWEEN YOU AND KIKYO?
...
LIKE SHE SAID... SHE TOOK THE SHIKON SHARD, AND ...
I'M SORRY.
THAT'S NOT WHAT I'M ASKING YOU!
DON'T TELL ME KIKYO...
...TRIED TO HURT YOU TOO...
...I CAN'T TELL HIM... I JUST CAN'T.
SHE ALMOST KILLED ME...

BUT SOMEHOW TELLING HIM....
...FEELS LIKE I'M TATTLING ON HER.
INU-YASHA...
YOU STILL...
...LOVE KIKYO. DON'T YOU ?
L...?
IS THIS ANY TIME TO TALK ABOUT *THAT*?!
WHAT ARE YOU GETTING SO DEFEN-SIVE ABOUT ?
YOU... IDIOT !!
IT'S BECAUSE I THOUGHT ABOUT *YOU* THAT I'M HERE RIGHT NOW!
...?

IF I HADN'T THOUGHT OF KAGOME AT THAT MOMENT...
...I'D HAVE BEEN POSSESSED...
KILLED BY KIKYO'S ILLUSION IN NARAKU'S TRAP.
INU-YASHA...
...PLEASE... TRY TO TRUST ME JUST A LITTLE BIT MORE?
SO WOULD YOU...
!
SKWEEZ
OH!
...ARE YOU TWO FINISHED FIGHTING?
...
WOBBLE

MY GOLEM HAS BEEN DESTROY-ED--
!
SHFF
YOU'VE BECOME CARELESS, NARAKU.
I CAN'T SEE ANY-THING--
NOT EVEN KIKYO'S WHERE-ABOUTS...

SHFF
KIKYO...
YOUR MAKESHIFT SPELLS HAVE NO POWER OVER ME.
REMEMBER THIS, NARAKU.
WAS CHILD'S PLAY FOR ME TO SUNDER.
EVEN THE SHIELD YOU RAISED AROUND THIS CASTLE TO PRE-VENT INU-YASHA AND THE OTHERS FROM FINDING IT--
GLEEM

TING
KLAKK
THE SHIKON SHARD ?!
IT'S WHAT YOU WANTED, ISN'T IT?
I'LL LET YOU BE ITS GUARDIAN.
FOR NOW... I SUSPECT YOU ARE THE ONE WHO MOST NEEDS IT...
...THE DEMON NARAKU.
OR, RATHER....

HSSH
...THE HALF-BREED NARAKU.
ONLY A HALF-BREED...?
YOU CALL ME...
BUT THE MORTAL AT THE HEART OF YOUR EXISTENCE...THE BANDIT WEAKLING ONIGUMO...HAS NOT BEEN ERASED.
AH, YES. YOU IMAGINE THAT YOU'VE SUPPRESSED IT WELL.

THAT'S WHY YOU CRAVE THE SHIKON JEWEL...
...THAT YOU MAY COMPLETE YOUR DEMONIC TRANS-FIGURATION.
IF THAT IS WHAT YOU THINK, WHY HAND ME THIS SHARD...?
I AM HE WHO FIFTY YEARS AGO MADE YOU SEEK YOUR OWN DEATH.
KNOWING THAT, YOU WOULD STILL...?
FEH.
THAT DAY...
MY BODY PER-ISHED...

BUT NOW...
ANIMATING THIS CONSTRUCT OF OTHERS' FLESH...
...I FEEL MORE ALIVE THAN EVER.
I CAN LOVE AND I CAN HATE...
MY SOUL IS FREER THAN IN ITS MORTALITY.
THEN... DOES SHE TRULY NOT SEEK MY DEATH...?
I WILL RETURN TO THE TEMPLE WHERE I LODGED BEFORE.
I WILL NOT BOLT OR HIDE.
IF YOU WISH TO MEET WITH ME, SEND A MESSENGER.
ONI-GUMO...
...

HSSHH
ONCE AGAIN... IT RISES UP.
THE BANDIT ONIGUMO'S BURN MARK... THE SPIDER ON MY BACK...WILL NOT DISAPPEAR...
NO MATTER HOW MANY TIMES I EXCHANGE BODIES...
YOU ARE A HALF-BREED, NARAKU...
KIKYO...

WHAT IS THAT WITCH SCHEMING?
I DON'T UNDER-STAND.
SHK
MY DEAR NARAKU... GO FORTH AND GATHER THE SHIKON SHARDS.
AND WHEN YOU HAVE FINALLY OBTAINED THE ENTIRE SHIKON JEWEL...
I WILL SEND YOU TO HELL.

HEY--
YOU BETTER NOT BE TRICKING ME, MYŌGA.
ARE YOU **SURE** THIS WHAT'S-HIS-NAME HAS MASTERED THE TETSUSAIGA?
HIS NAME IS LORD INU-YASHA!
INU-YASHA, EH... ?
SKRITCH SKRITCH
THE DOG-DEMON WHO GAVE ME HIS FANG TO HONE INTO A SWORD HAD A PAIR OF WHELPS...
THIS MUST BE THE YOUNGER OF THE TWO IDIOT BROTHERS.
MM.

...BUT WITH A SINGLE SWING HE SLAUGHTERED A HORDE OF DEMONS.
I SAW IT HAPPEN ONLY ONCE...
HE'S DANGEROUS TO BE AROUND, ALL RIGHT....
PHEW
HE'S DONE NOTHING LIKE IT IN MY PRESENCE SINCE... LUCKILY.
SEE IF THIS INU-YASHA CUR...
WELL, I'LL TEST HIM SURE ENOUGH.
...IS REALLY WORTHY OF WIELDING MY FINE-EDGED MASTERPIECE!

SCROLL SEVEN

TOTO-SAI, THE SWORDSMITH

OW!
HOT! HOT!
ARRRH— I CAN'T STAND THIS PLACE!
EVEN THE SOIL IS HOT!
ARE YOU THERE, TŌTŌ-SAI?!

TODAY'S THE DAY YOU PROMISED IT!
YOU'D BETTER HAVE FINISHED FORGING THAT BLADE WE ORDERED!
OH!
I HAVE MOVED
TŌTŌ-SAI!
I'M SO SORRY, LORD SESSHŌ-MARU!
GROVEL GROVEL
SO TŌTŌ-SAI HAS FLED, EH?
MMM...

THESE ARTISTIC GENIUSES, YOU KNOW, THEY HAVE SUCH VOLATILE PERSONALI-TIES...
I'VE HEARD THAT ANY TIME HE DOESN'T THINK HIS CLIENT WILL TRULY APPRECIATE HIS ART, HE'LL JUST UP AND--
THEN YOU ARE SAYING...
...THAT HE FEELS THAT I AM NOT **WORTHY** OF ONE OF HIS BLADES?!
HISS
ER--
HOW CAN I SAY THIS...?
I THINK IT'S JUST A MATTER OF **PERSONAL PREFERENCE.**
BOP
AARGH!

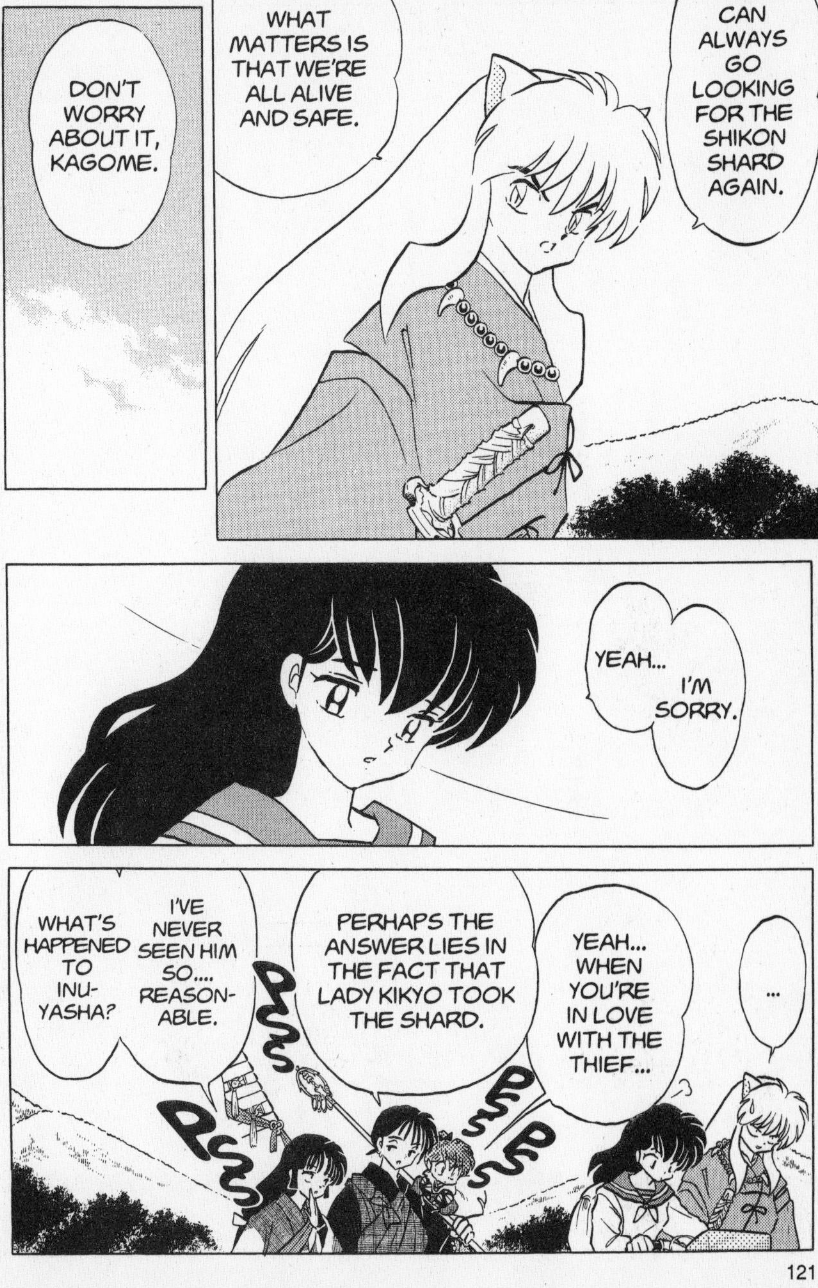

DON'T WORRY ABOUT IT, KAGOME.
WHAT MATTERS IS THAT WE'RE ALL ALIVE AND SAFE.
WE CAN ALWAYS GO LOOKING FOR THE SHIKON SHARD AGAIN.
YEAH... I'M SORRY.
WHAT'S HAPPENED TO INU-YASHA?
I'VE NEVER SEEN HIM SO.... REASON-ABLE.
PERHAPS THE ANSWER LIES IN THE FACT THAT LADY KIKYO TOOK THE SHARD.
YEAH... WHEN YOU'RE IN LOVE WITH THE THIEF...
...

—STARE
WH- WHAT?!
KAGOME, NOT YOU TOO...
DON'T TELL ME YOU THINK I'M COVERING FOR KIKYO!
AREN'T YOU?
NOW LISTEN,
YOU--!
WHOOSH
EH?!
WHOA!

PAPAH!!
WHA?!

WHO THE HELL ARE YOU?!

MY NAME IS TŌTŌ-SAI.
DRAW YOUR BLADE, INU-YASHA.
THIS CREATURE... KNOWS ME?!
VYOOO
IF YOU WON'T DRAW FIRST... THEN I'LL HAVE TO!

STAND BACK, KAGOME!
SHHH
O-OK!
KLANG
UNH!
HE'S FORCING THE TETSUSAIGA BACK?!
ZZZ

TUP
WHA...?
HMPH. ITS SHEEN IS STILL MURKY.
BLONG
TING
WHAT THE HELL ARE YOU?!
VOOSH
!
SLAP

HE STOPPED THE "WOLF'S FANG"... WITH A PIECE OF HIDE?!
OH...!
THERE'S SOMETHING BIZARRE HERE...
DON'T YOU KNOW HOW TO TAKE CARE OF A SWORD?!
WAAUGH! AND LOOK AT ALL THOSE NICKS ON THE BLADE!
GRNN GRNN
OLD MAN MYŌGA!
PINNG
TŌTŌ-SAI! THAT'S ENOUGH!
YES, LORD INU-YASHA.
SO THIS...
GEEZER... IS THE SMITH WHO FORGED THE TETSUSAIGA?!

INDEED. IT WAS I WHO TEMPERED THIS LEGENDARY WEAPON FROM YOUR FATHER'S FANG.
WOW.
SO, WHAT BUSINESS DOES HE HAVE WITH ME? DID YOU COME TO SHARPEN THE BLADE OR SOMETHING?
EXACTLY... IF YOU ARE TRULY WORTHY TO WIELD SUCH A SWORD.
HOWEVER...
IF YOU ARE UNWORTHY... I SHALL BREAK THE TETSUSAIGA MYSELF!
WHAT?!
ARE YOU SAYING THIS IS SOME KIND OF TEST...?
GZABE

QUITE.
I AM A HUNTED MAN.
HUNTED--?
"FORGE ME A BLADE THAT WILL RIVAL TETSUSAIGA.
OTHERWISE I SHALL KILL YOU."
THERE'S AN IDIOT OUT THERE SPOUTING SUCH NONSENSE.
YOU HAVE TO PROTECT ME FROM HIM.
LISTEN, OLD MAN...
DON'T YOU MEAN, "PLEASE PROTECT ME FROM HIM"...?
HE'S HERE!
WHA--?

OH...!
AWK--!
WAFT
TP...
SHK

SESSHŌ-MARU...
WHAT? WHO'S HE?!
INU-YASHA'S ELDER BROTHER....
INU-YASHA....
WHY ARE **YOU** CONSORTING WITH TŌTŌ-SAI?
HSSS
UM... YOU MEAN THE PERSON WHO'S THREATENING YOUR LIFE IS...
MM-HM. THAT'S HIM.

HE'S GOING TO PROTECT ME!
DUCK
HO.
YOU REALLY MUST...
HISS
KRAK
...DESIRE THE GRAVE.
BUT WAIT!
IF YOU DEFEAT INU-YASHA, THEN I WILL FORGE YOU A NEW BLADE!
HEY!
...
THAT WAS A QUICK CHANGE!
"CHANGE"...?
HMMM?
TŌTŌ-SAI....
YOU WILL NOT FORGET THOSE WORDS.
!

YOU HEARD HIM, INU-YASHA! YOU MUST DIE!
GYAH!
PAH! I'LL THROW THOSE WORDS BACK AT YOU!
WHY CAN'T BROTHERS GET ALONG?
YOU DIDN'T EXACTLY **HELP**!

SCROLL EIGHT

TENSEIGA

NOW---!

!
PFF
BWOK
YOW!

WHAT'S THE TROUBLE, INU-YASHA?
FOOSH
I THOUGHT YOU WERE GOING TO DEFEAT ME TO SAVE TŌTŌ-SAI!
UNGH!
YOU'RE AS SLOW AS EVER.
TRY THIS!
HROOO

HMPH... NOT EVEN A SCRATCH.
Tp
!
HE HAS MASTERED IT!
MYŌGA! I THOUGHT YOU SAID INU-YASHA HAD MASTERED THAT SWORD!
WELL... I SAID HE DID ONCE...
IN THE END, HE ALWAYS BEATS SESSHŌ-MARU!
AND EVERY TIME THEY FIGHT...
JUST MY LUCK...
A COMPLETE INCOMPETENT!

GLARE
AIEE- HE'S LOOKING THIS WAY!
DUCK
DEAR TŌTŌSAI...
DON'T YOU THINK THIS IS A WASTE?
INU-YASHA'S SWINGING THE BLADE AROUND WITH BRUTE STRENGTH.
YOUR MASTER BLADE MIGHT AS WELL BE A LOG.
HEY, WHAT ARE YOU NODDING ABOUT?!
SIGH... IT'S TRUE!
FEH!
YOU DON'T KNOW ANYTHING, OLD COWARD!
THIS BATTLE'S JUST BEGUN!
PREPARE TO DIE!
HROOO

KRAK KRAK
THE END WILL BE THE SAME NO MATTER HOW MANY TIMES YOU STRIKE.
BRILLIANT VENOM CLAWS!
GRAB
WILL YOU FORGE A BLADE FOR ME NOW?!
WELL, TŌTŌ-SAI?!
UMM...

PWFF
NOPE!
WHAT?!
!

LIAR!
WHAT THE HELL DO YOU THINK YOU'RE DOING?!
BWOK
HHOOO
SO YOU'LL REFUSE ME REGARDLESS?
?!
DID YOU FORGET?
I'VE ALREADY GIVEN YOU A SPLENDID BLADE OF YOUR OWN?!

THE TENSEIGA THAT IS AT YOUR HIP!
I FORGED IT TOO FROM YOUR MUTUAL FATHER'S FANG!
IT TOO IS A MASTER BLADE! FINER PERHAPS EVEN THAN TETSUSAIGA!!
SESSHŌ-MARU'S BLADE WAS ALSO FORGED BY THE OLD MAN...?
BUT WE'VE NEVER SEEN HIM DRAW IT.
"GIVE TENSEIGA TO THE ELDER SON, TETSUSAIGA TO THE YOUNGER"...
THAT WAS YOUR FATHER'S LAST WISH!
YOU CLAIM THIS BLUNT SLAB OF METAL IS WORTHY OF ME?
DON'T TRY TO PLAY WITH ME, TŌTŌ-SAI.
HHSSS

WHAT...
HOI
HE'S GETTING MAD... MAYBE WE SHOULD GO.
BISH BISH
GYAH! LAVA!!
GASP GASP

THEY GOT AWAY.
HMPH...
...
HHRRRR
GLUB GLUB
YOU DON'T REALLY NEED INU-YASHA TO PROTECT YOU, DO YOU?
INDEED...
WOW-- YOU'RE PRETTY STRONG....

SIGH—
I MISPLACED MY HOPES.
I DIDN'T THINK INU-YASHA WAS **THIS** WEAK.
WHAT?!
AND SESSHŌ-MARU CALLS MY MASTER BLADE A "SLAB"...
SIGH
...OUCH!
WHO ARE YOU CALLING **WEAK**?!
I NEVER REALIZED...
THAT THE SWORD AT YOUR SIDE IS AN HEIRLOOM FROM YOUR LORD FATHER.
JUST WHAT SORT OF DEMON BLADE IS IT?
...DO YOU REALLY WANT TO KNOW, JAKEN?

ZHOOO
EH?!
ARE YOU A FOOL?
GET UP.
HSSS
LORD...
SESSHŌ-MARU...?
THUD

BUT...
I'M...
I'M NOT INJURED?
WHY?!
I COULD HAVE SWORN I WAS SPLIT IN HALF
DO YOU UNDER-STAND NOW?
THIS TENSEIGA...
IS A BLADE THAT DOES NOT KILL.
A BLADE THAT CAN'T CUT--?
SO HOW ARE YOU SUPPOSED TO FIGHT WITH IT?

TENSEIGA IS NOT A BLADE TO FIGHT WITH.
IT IS A BLADE OF HEALING.
HOOOO
HEALING?!
UNLIKE TETSUSAIGA, FORGED TO DESTROY THE STRONG...
TENSEIGA BINDS TOGETHER THE UNRAVELING SOULS OF THOSE WHO ARE WEAK.
BINDS... SOULS...?
THEN... CAN IT BRING SOULS BACK FROM DEATH...?
IF YOU MASTER IT.
IF YOU HAVE A SOUL THAT TREASURES LIFE,
THEN YOU'D BE ABLE TO SAVE EVEN A HUNDRED SOULS WITH A SINGLE SWING OF TENSEIGA.
A LOVING SOUL....

I SEE NOW.
NO WONDER THAT BASTARD SESSHŌ-MARU WANTS A NEW BLADE.
HE'D NEVER BE ABLE TO USE A BLADE LIKE THAT. NOT IF HE STOOD ON HIS HEAD!
I SUPPOSE NOT.
NOT WITH HIS ATTITUDE, NO.
AND EVEN IF HE **COULD** USE IT, HE PROBABLY WOULDN'T BE HAPPY ABOUT IT.
HHSSS
HAVE THERE EVER BEEN STUPIDER BANDITS?

EVEN TO CONTEMPLATE ASSAULTING THE MIGHTY LORD SESSHŌ-MARU....
...
IF THAT SENILE FOOL...
... WILL NOT FORGE ME A BLADE, I HAVE NO FURTHER USE FOR HIM.
I'LL SEND HIM TO THE NEXT REALM....
HIM AND MY LITTLE BROTHER BOTH.

SCROLL NINE

SCAR OF THE WIND

WHAT DO YOU MEAN, THIS IS WHERE WE PART...?
ARE YOU PLANNING TO ESCAPE ON YOUR OWN?
MM. I CAN'T RELY ON INU-YASHA.
WELL THEN...
BUT...
LET HIM GO, KAGOME.
WE DON'T HAVE ANY **USE** FOR THE OLD GEEZER, ANYWAY.
POMP

GIVE IT BACK.
EH?
GNNG
YOU CAN'T USE TETSUSAIGA PROPERLY.
SO I'M GOING TO DE-STROY IT.
HEY, INU-YASHA!
DOMF
NO MORE JOKES, OLD FOOL.
YOU'LL REGRET THIS--!
KLOP KLOP KLOP KLOP
HE'S A STRAIGHT-FORWARD FIGHTER...
BUT IS THAT A STRENGTH OR A WEAKNESS?
POOR INU-YASHA. I DO FEEL SORRY FOR HIM...
KLOP KLOP KLOP KLOP KLOP
HE'LL DIE AT SESSHŌ-MARU'S HANDS.

IT SEEMS THAT HE HASN'T EVEN SENSED THE "SCAR OF THE WIND"...
...THAT DRAWS OUT THE TRUE POWER OF TETSUSAIGA!
YOU DON'T WANT TO FOLLOW HIM, INU-YASHA?
I MEAN, YOU FINALLY GOT TO MEET YOUR SWORD'S CREATOR....
THAT SENILE OLD FOOL....!
KLOP KLOP KLOP KLOP KLOP KLOP
HUH?
HE'S COMING BACK...?
!

DID YOU REALLY THINK YOU COULD ESCAPE ME...?
TŌTŌ-SAI...
SIZZZLE
SESSHŌ-MARU...!

FEH.
SO HE SAYS. WHAT ARE YOU GOING TO DO?
ZIP
OLD MAN, DO YOU HAVE ANY INTENTION OF FORGING SESSHŌ-MARU A NEW BLADE?
SEE?
NOPE.
I'LL TEAR YOU TO SHREDS... TOGETHER WITH INU-YASHA.
JUST WAIT THERE.
KRAK

AND I'M GETTING PRETTY TIRED OF BEING **LECTURED** ABOUT THIS SWORD... SO...
LET'S **DECIDE** THIS ONCE AND FOR ALL-- **RIGHT NOW!**
AS YOU WISH.
WE'LL FINISH IT TODAY.

WHOA!
TAKE THIS!

WH-WHAT'S THAT ARM?!
OH...!
HE'S ATTACHED A REPLACEMENT ARM!
THE LEFT ARM THAT INU-YASHA SEVERED...
BUT IF IT'S ANOTHER DEMON'S ARM...
THE TETSUSAIGA SHOULD BE ABLE TO FIGHT IT...

HAVE YOU FORGOTTEN, BROTHER?!
THE TETSUSAIGA'S SHIELD REPELS YOU!
FEH...

!
I'VE FORGOTTEN NOTHING.
FWSH
UGH...!
VZZZ

THIS NEW ARM...
...WILL SERVE AS A SHIELD AGAINST THE BLADE'S AURA.
KRAK KRAK
WHAT...?
THAT'S... A **DRAGON'S** LIMB.
FAR TOUGHER THAN ANY DEMON'S ARM....
HMPH! IT TOOK QUITE A GASH FROM JUST **ONE BLOW** OF MY BLADE!
YES.
AS IT SHOULD HAVE...

OR DO YOU NOT KNOW OF THE "SCAR OF THE WIND"?!
?!
WHAT?!
NNGH!
BZT
BZT
BZT
ZMMM

I HAVE NO NEED TO FEAR...
...THE TETSUSAIGA WIELDED BY ONE SO UNAWARE!
RGH!
UNH!
HE'S PARRYING THE TETSUSAIGA WITH JUST ONE ARM?!
HIS IS A POWERFUL EVIL...!
!

SSHHH
RRR--!
GRRNN
INU-YASHA!
TP
SESSHŌ-MARU...!
YOU CAN SENSE THE SCAR OF THE WIND?!

...
SIR... WHAT'S THIS "SCAR OF THE WIND"...?
...
IT IS THE SECRET TO MASTERING THE TETSUSAIGA.
IS THE PROPER *PATH* THAT DRAWS OUT A BLADE'S TRUE POWER.
OF COURSE!
SO COULD ANYONE WITH HIS EYES OPEN.

BUT THAT PATH IS NOT SOMETHING THAT CAN BE TAUGHT.
NOR IS IT SOMETHING ONE CAN SEE WITH THE EYES...
"SENSE THE SCAR OF THE WIND..."?
WHAT THE HELL DOES THAT MEAN?!

SCROLL TEN

THE INVISIBLE PATH

...WHAT THIS "SCAR OF THE WIND" IS....
I DON'T EVEN KNOW...
HOOO
...AND SESSHŌ-MARU CAN SEE IT?!

IF THIS "SCAR" IS THE SECRET TO MASTERING THE TETSUSAIGA...
THEN PLEASE TEACH IT TO INU-YASHA!
BUT...
THAT IS NOT POSSIBLE.
INU-YASHA MUST MASTER IT ON HIS OWN.
HMPH.
I'VE *NEVER* UNDERSTOOD...
IF HE CANNOT...
...THEN IT MEANS THAT INU-YASHA WAS NEVER MEANT TO WIELD THE TETSUSAIGA AFTER ALL.
BRAK

WHAT WOULD POSSESS SUCH A FINE BLADE...
TO CHOOSE *YOU* AS ITS OWNER?!
NKH...!
THE SCAR OF THE WIND...
HOW IS IT MY HALF-BROTHER CAN SEE IT, BUT I CAN'T?!
W... WAIT...
LAST TIME... WHEN SESSHŌ-MARU SHOWED UP WITH A HUMAN ARM ATTACHED...

HE HANDILY SLAUGHTERED A HUNDRED DEMONS AT ONCE.
UHHH!
THAT SLICE... THAT SPACE... IS THAT THE "SCAR"?!
WITH JUST ONE SWING...
...SLICING THE VERY AIR BEFORE THEM...

EH?!
FUMP
ROLL
I'M FEELING... SUDDENLY WEAK!
INU-YASHA?!
IS IT YOUR INJURY--?!
HEH. EARLIER, I GAVE YOU A GOOD TASTE ...
...OF THE VENOM IN WHICH MY TALONS ARE STEEPED.
SSSS...
THE MORE YOU MOVE, THE MORE THE VENOM CIRCULATES!
NNH!
AUGH!

I CAN'T TAKE STAND BY AND WATCH THIS ANY MORE!
SANGO!
BOOMERANG BONE!
OH...!

DON'T YOU DARE INTERFERE!
VMMMM
SESSHŌ-MARU IS MINE...
...TO DEFEAT WITH THE TETSUSAIGA!

BUT, INU-YASHA...
JUST STAND BACK AND WATCH, SANGO.
REMEMBER, INU-YASHA DID MASTER THE SWORD... EVEN IF ONLY ONCE.
THAT WAS AN ACCIDENT AND YOU KNOW IT!
PERHAPS IT WAS...
BUT IF HE LACKED THE SKILL HE WOULD NOT HAVE BEEN ABLE TO ACCOMPLISH IT.
BUT...
IF HE CAN'T MASTER IT RIGHT HERE, RIGHT NOW... HE'LL BE KILLED!
B-DMP B-DMP B-DMP
YOU WILL REGRET TURNING DOWN MY OFFER OF ASSISTANCE, INU-YASHA!
WAFT

SHUT UP!
I'LL FIND THAT "SCAR OF THE WIND"!
SURRENDER!
GRAB
BZZT BZZT
IF HE CAN SEE IT...
...THEN SO CAN I!!

I WILL NOT...
...LOSE TO YOU--!
THE DRAGON'S ARM...!
OH...!

SUCH A WASTE...
WOK
SUCH FUTILE STRUGGLE...
FUB
!
ZSH
THE VENOM...!
I... I CAN'T SEE!!

BWOK
BASH
BASH
BASH
BASH
OH...!

SSSHHH...
UNGH...
SSS...
INU-YASHA... HIS EYES...!
WAS HE BLINDED...?!
YOU AND I...
...ARE SIMPLY NOT IN THE SAME CLASS.
KRIK

YOU DIRTY LITTLE HALF-BREED!
HE'S SHOWING HIS REAL FEATURES!
H-HIS FACE--!
HE'S APPROACHING...

I CAN FEEL IT... THE SWIRLING MIASMA. HIS DEMONIC POWER...
HOOO
THE HEAT OF WIND STRIKING WIND...
WHERE THE POWERS SWIRL AND COLLIDE–
THE SMELL OF THE AIR...
IT'S DIFFERENT!
!

HOOOO
THERE'S A SPACE BETWEEN. AN OPENING... I CAN SMELL IT!

TO BE CONTINUED...

About Rumiko Takahashi

Born in 1957 in Niigata, Japan, Rumiko Takahashi attended women's college in Tokyo, where she began studying comics with Kazuo Koike, author of *Crying Freeman*. She later became an assistant to horror-manga artist Kazuo Umezu (*Orochi*). In 1978, she won a prize in Shogakukan's annual "New Comic Artist Contest," and in that same year her boy-meets-alien comedy series *Urusei Yatsura* began appearing in the weekly manga magazine *Shônen Sunday*. This phenomenally successful series ran for nine years and sold over 22 million copies. Takahashi's later *Ranma 1/2* series enjoyed even greater popularity.

Takahashi is considered by many to be one of the world's most popular manga artists. With the publication of Volume 34 of her *Ranma 1/2* series in Japan, Takahashi's total sales passed *one hundred million* copies of her compiled works.

Takahashi's serial titles include *Urusei Yatsura, Ranma 1/2, One-Pound Gospel, Maison Ikkoku* and *InuYasha*. Additionally, Takahashi has drawn many short stories which have been published in America under the title "Rumic Theater," and several installments of a saga known as her "Mermaid" series. Most of Takahashi's major stories have also been animated, and are widely available in translation worldwide. *InuYasha* is her most recent serial story, first published in *Shônen Sunday* in 1996.

COMPLETE OUR SURVEY AND LET US KNOW WHAT YOU THINK!

☐ Please check here if you DO NOT wish to receive information or future offers from VIZ

Name: ______________________________

Address: ______________________________

City: ______________ **State:** ________ **Zip:** ______________

E-mail: ______________________________

☐ **Male** ☐ **Female** **Date of Birth** (mm/dd/yyyy): ___/___/______ (**Under 13? Parental consent required**)

What race/ethnicity do you consider yourself? (please check one)

☐ Asian/Pacific Islander ☐ Black/African American ☐ Hispanic/Latino

☐ Native American/Alaskan Native ☐ White/Caucasian ☐ Other: ________

What VIZ product did you purchase? (check all that apply and indicate title purchased)

☐ DVD/VHS ______________________________

☐ Graphic Novel ______________________________

☐ Magazines ______________________________

☐ Merchandise ______________________________

Reason for purchase: (check all that apply)

☐ Special offer ☐ Favorite title ☐ Gift

☐ Recommendation ☐ Other ______________

Where did you make your purchase? (please check one)

☐ Comic store ☐ Bookstore ☐ Mass/Grocery Store

☐ Newsstand ☐ Video/Video Game Store ☐ Other: ________

☐ Online (site: ______________________________)

What other VIZ properties have you purchased/own? ______________________________

____

How many anime and/or manga titles have you purchased in the last year? How many were VIZ titles? (please check one from each column)

ANIME	MANGA	VIZ
☐ None	☐ None	☐ None
☐ 1-4	☐ 1-4	☐ 1-4
☐ 5-10	☐ 5-10	☐ 5-10
☐ 11+	☐ 11+	☐ 11+

I find the pricing of VIZ products to be: (please check one)

☐ Cheap ☐ Reasonable ☐ Expensive

What genre of manga and anime would you like to see from VIZ? (please check two)

☐ Adventure ☐ Comic Strip ☐ Science Fiction ☐ Fighting

☐ Horror ☐ Romance ☐ Fantasy ☐ Sports

What do you think of VIZ's new look?

☐ Love It ☐ It's OK ☐ Hate It ☐ Didn't Notice ☐ No Opinion

Which do you prefer? (please check one)

☐ Reading right-to-left

☐ Reading left-to-right

Which do you prefer? (please check one)

☐ Sound effects in English

☐ Sound effects in Japanese with English captions

☐ Sound effects in Japanese only with a glossary at the back

THANK YOU! Please send the completed form to:

NJW Research
42 Catharine St.
Poughkeepsie, NY 12601

All information provided will be used for internal purposes only. We promise not to sell or otherwise divulge your information.